IGNITE

Raise Your Energy in 30 Seconds or Less Naturally So You SHINE With More Confidence, Joy And Abundance!

For you
AJ

IGNITE

Raise Your Energy in 30 Seconds or Less Naturally So You SHINE With More Confidence, Joy And Abundance!

Keep Igniting your Gifts

I love you

"☺"
Angel

ANGEL MARIE MONACHELLI

You Inspire ME...
& SO MANY oThers!

Paperback ISBN: 978-0-9977341-7-1

Table of Contents

What They Are Saying About Ignite

When I think of Angel Marie, I think of a ray of sunshine! From the moment we connected, I felt this unexplainable Energy. Something I had never felt. Angel knows how to extract that Energy from others and touches everyone's heart in the process. Angel has touched my life and helped me become a better version of myself. Her story will make you laugh, cry, and, most of all, SHINE!

~ Emilio & Daniela Roman, CEO Co-Author Network/
Millionaire Academy, LLC

"You bring such healing to humanity, and I love this book! I am so grateful for your Reiki Energy Healing and guidance all these years. Angel, you truly are a gift from above."

~ Barbara Anderson

"Angel is a shining example of exuding positivity no matter what is going on. The world needs more leaders like her. She's a breath of fresh air and always an inspiration. I am honored to have written her "Shine On" song."

~ FiZ Singer/Songwriter

"This book has brilliant tips to help women discover new ways to raise their energy and take inspired action with joy."

~ Sophia Olivas CEO of EverSmart City,
2X Best Selling Author, Speaker

"Angel's uplifting energy is infectious and this book channels that energy to you on every page."

~ Preston Martelly Best Selling Author,
Speaker & Digital Nomad

"Who knew that something as simple as taking a deep breath, or noticing the feel of the sun on my skin, or my bare feet in the grass would be what I needed to shift my Energy and the way my day was going? Angel Marie, that's who! The golden nuggets that Angel Marie shares in this book are quick and easy to do and will significantly change your life!"

~ Dr. Sony Jackson, Best Selling Author,
Marketing Strategist & Empire Builder

"This book helps increase your positive Energy towards a more inspired lifestyle. I love the insights and easy tips. Keep Shining Angel!"

~ Aaron Heimes, President and Co-Founder, e360tv

"In 2009, I was widowed and had no direction in my life; I was blessed to meet Angel. After one Reiki session with her, my physical and emotional pain was gone. I had clarity once again. Under Angel's healing wings, I became a Reiki Master, and her coaching and books inspire me to live my truth and be of service to others every day."

~ M. Simmons. RMT, LAA, Ht, OM

"Viewers watching her television show can sense her vibrant Energy out in TVland, which is needed in the world. This book reveals her positive Energy. I highly recommend Angel's book. Thank you for sharing your expertise and tips."

~ Jim Grant, TV & Radio Producer and Host

"Angel is who I have entrusted to be my Reiki Master. Thank you for helping me to understand and navigate my gifts. You are light!"

~ Shawn Jones, CEO INETrepreneur Network

"If you want someone to energize and improve your life quickly, read this book. Her contagious energy delivers results!"

~ Tim Burt "America's Number One Marketing Strategist"

"You'll be delighted with the positive changes in your life when you incorporate Angel's valuable, easy-to-use techniques from this remarkable book. She is an Energy expert who shares what works based on her extensive knowledge and experience. I am immensely grateful for the many constructive results I've experienced using Angel's simple, concrete steps to shift my Energy quickly."

~ Lynn W. Murphy, M.Ed.
Founder of Women Who Push the Limits

"Ignite Book has helped open my eyes to the unique ways Energy is perceived. Angel's teachings have helped change my life and raise my Energy, and I now live a life of Abundance; thank you, Angel."

~ Tami E. Mullen, Lightworker

"Ignite!" is the best new inspirational self-help book I've read! It's a page-turner, but you should read it slowly and absorb every technique. You will learn how to Ignite your own Energy and enjoy every aspect, every minute of your life! Thank you, Angel Marie, for being my Reiki Master/Teacher.

~ Linda Mardel, Reiki Master, Writer & Traveler

Foreword

In this book, the listener on the path to healing, joy, and success will, without a doubt, be inspired by Angel Marie's pure awareness and direct knowledge.

Angel Marie's wisdom, tips, and lessons will guide you and assist you on your journey to SHINE your brightest and most authentic self!

Her writing emits light within itself; in her very soulful and genuine approach, you will feel she is right next to you as you read it. What a gift to the body, mind, and soul!

This book is essential to your personal development and spiritual ascension. As you experience its genius, you will feel joy and abundance closer than you ever imagined with the confidence to take action!

Juju- Creator of Biztuition
Host of The Mystical Entrepreneur.com

Meet Angel Marie:
"I have almost died 4 times."

Family legend has it that Angel Marie has been a joyful ray of sunshine from the moment she entered this world. And it's true, as children, we are most connected to our intuition, Energy, and joy. We see the world through eyes filled with wonder and appreciation, always looking for the beauty, good, and connection.

Despite being labeled as "stupid" because of dyslexia; being told she would not make it through high school, let alone college, despite being sexually molested, Angel Marie continued to Shine her light in the world and persisted through high school and college.

Her work experiences have run the gamut from being a dishwasher in a pizza joint, a yacht mechanic, and owning five businesses to being a counselor/coach and a speaker. Then, one transformational year, she experienced a financial and emotional collapse, losing both a business and a relationship during the height of the recession. From these experiences, she learned the effects of stress and trauma on the body directly: being diagnosed with lupus, fibromyalgia, arthritis, and Sjögren's disease, which led her to the discovery of the power of Reiki Energy Healing.

Once she learned and connected with the healing power of Energy, nutrition, and mindset, she made a commitment to spend her life sharing her positive Energy with everyone she meets. She teaches how to Ignite joy, love, and peace together on this life adventure so that everyone can step into better health and more Energy and claim financial freedom.

Being a naturally high Energy person, she enjoys putting herself in situations where the natural Energy of the world flows uninhibited, like camping, hiking, and swimming at the lake, and where she can flow with the Energy, like dancing and practicing the art of Tai Chi.

As an Energy practitioner, she is a Reiki Master, conducts Reiki Energy Healing sessions, teaches others how to heal others and themselves with Reiki Energy Healing, and holds retreats in the mountains surrounding Phoenix with a select handful of students.

She resides in her desert oasis, Phoenix, Arizona, with her best friend and companion, Shine.

I Wrote This Book for You!

The curiosity and resilience of humanity have always intrigued and inspired me. So, as I celebrate six decades of being on this planet, I deeply feel compassion for all humanity.

I have struggled in the past, and even today, when chronic physical pain is high, I experience negative self-talk. This leads to emotional overeating, self-sabotaging actions, low Energy, and feelings of apathy. However, these breakdowns, as I like to call them, create opportunities for breakthroughs.

I wrote this book to share my experiences and perception of life to guide you and give you tools of resilience to get you through those tough times. *Ignite* will help you recognize the wonderful, unique person you truly are.

I'm not saying I have all the answers. At first glance, the invitations in this book may seem random, and you will wonder how they could Ignite your Energy. I ask you to look beyond your limiting beliefs, dive deep with your open mind, and try some of these golden nuggets.

It's time to talk about ENERGY and how your Energy matters, how your Energy is the key to creating self-care, self-confidence, self-realization, joy, and abundance in every action. Everything is in life because everything is ENERGY!

Every activity we do requires Energy. This book will help you shift your perception of many activities to fill you with the Energy of peace, clarity, success, and balance.

I feel so comforted by the gifts that I can share. I believe that all of us coming together and discovering that we can raise our Energy in 30 seconds or less naturally in any place, in any situation, will ripple out positive Energy to the entire world.

Now it is time for you to truly connect to the difference between struggling every day and happily living a life of ease, grace, and glory.

Let's go on this adventure together!

Angel Marie

Change Your Mindset

CHANGE YOUR MINDSET

is coming from your headset and getting out of your head to understand the awareness of your life. It means changing the past loops that keep creating self-sabotage and the feeling of being stuck.

IGNITE YOUR LIFE

means moving to the heartset and connecting to what you are responsible for in your life. And, it's also choosing how you want to show up for others in your life.

AND SHINE ON!

means moving to the gutset and taking inspired action to create the life you desire and deserve!

When your headset, heartset and gutset are aligned, your Energy will flow to create a never-ending chain of love, light and healing that Shines bright in the whole world.

Raise Your Energy in 30 Seconds or Less Naturally.

The Shine On! Message

I celebrate you and the beautiful, shining Energy that you bring to the world.

In this book, you will learn that everything is Energy, frequency, and vibration. Shine On Energy helps you awaken your inner genius and raise your individual vibration (Energy). This is a powerful and needed Energy boost to help the world; it ALWAYS begins with you!

When you raise your Energy positively, studies show that your vibrational field will affect those around you; your family, friends, and community will be energized and pass their Energy along, causing a ripple effect that impacts the world for the better.

Thank you for being here and becoming part of the Shine On vibe.

Use the S.H.I.N.E. On Pledge to remind yourself to Shine. You will experience greater freedom, creativity, and self-expression.

The Shine On Pledge

S Smile Bright

H Heal With Breathing

I Ignite Your Laughter

N Nurture Your Health

E Energize Your Life

11 Quick Energy Boosts

Choose one of the activities below and do it non-stop for 30 seconds, and watch your Energy Ignite!

1. Clap Your Hands

2. Gently Tap Your Whole Entire Body

3. Scream And Yell

4. Ring A Bell

5. Laugh Out Loud

6. Get Up And Do The Shine On Shake

7. Smile Bright

8. Dance

9. Go Outside

10. Take Deep Diaphragmatic Breaths

11. Make Yourself Yawn

Chapter 1 Health Energy

Have you ever said, "I am healthy," or "I have good health," or have you asked yourself, "Do I have good health?" "Am I healthy?" What is good health? How do we create good health? How do we have a healthy lifestyle? Now that I have you thinking, here's to exploring different ways to raise your Energy naturally while creating a healthy body and lifestyle.

"Amazing wellness is created by a healthy mind and proper physical alignment." ~ Angel Marie

Water Energy

Do you like water? What kind of water do you drink? Do you have water right next to you ready to drink? Are you challenged with trying to remember to drink more water? Have you ever said, "I'm not thirsty; I don't need to drink water?"

Water is our lifeline. Water nurtures the cells, helps lubricate the muscles, and balances brain function. The benefits are tremendous. Many studies say that even 1% to 3% of dehydration causes decreased brain function and lack of clarity. Many healthcare studies say to drink at least half your weight in ounces of water a day.

Action Step from the SHINE ON! book

Breathe... Measure your weight in pounds. Cut that number in half. This number is how many ounces of water are recommended per day. Celebrate your water intake! And breathe...

There are common complaints about not drinking enough water. Has this ever happened to you? You experience brain fog and low Energy, and the biggest one is feeling more pain throughout your body. Water is Energy! Water also reminds us to stay in the flow of life.

Another study showed that it matters what kind of water you are drinking. So, I invite you to look at your water source and determine what the best water to drink is. I recommend mountain spring water to get more nutrients to my counseling clients and Reiki students, yet I am not a certified nutritionist or doctor, so please look up what is the best water for you to drink.

Raise your Energy within 30 seconds or less naturally by drinking more water. Feel better and have more clarity!

Diaphragmatic Breathing Energy

Do you find yourself holding your breath? Are you a shallow breather? Do you get dizzy when you take a deep breath? Do you have a breathing practice?

Diaphragmatic breathing is an amazingly healthy way to heal your body. Diaphragmatic breathing is an ancient practice that has become popular since the 1970s. Studies have shown that it helps to balance your Energy, gives you a greater sense of mental clarity, and improves your body's immune system. This is because every system relies on oxygen. In addition, it helps to reduce stress levels and anxiety.

I did a study with my Reiki students and asked them to take three diaphragmatic deep breaths every hour on the hour. They reported to me that on the days they did that throughout the day, they had more Energy and motivation. They also had a sense of calm, control, and safety. Those days were so unlike the days when they did not do the breaths, when they felt increased worry and mind chatter.

Action Step from the SHINE ON! Book

Breathe... Every time you go to the bathroom, take three deep breaths. Leave your phone in another room. And breathe...

 The health benefits of taking a deep diaphragmatic breath are huge. I encourage you to learn diaphragmatic breathing and adapt it to your daily life. Watch my video on YouTube and save your life by taking a deep breath. Do it NOW! You got this!

Raise your Energy in 30 seconds or less naturally by taking a diaphragmatic breath!

Sleep Energy

Do you have insomnia? Do you toss and turn at night? Does your brain never shut off? Do your feet hurt so badly that you can't sleep? Do you feel like you're dragging around your physical body and that every day is a struggle?

Sleep is Energy. Sleep time varies for every human being on the planet, so I'm not going to declare how much sleep you're supposed to get. The average human gets at least 6 to 8 hours. I am not a healthcare specialist. I am an example of a 60 plus year old with high Energy, enthusiasm, and joy for life. This is because I put sleep as a high priority.

I conducted a survey online, and the results were shocking. Most people do not sleep more than four hours a night and feel stuck and overwhelmed in their life. There are many theories, from new age doctrines to spiritual and religious views, as well as scientific and medical studies on sleep. When you sleep, you are helping your body's Energy to clear, cleanse and relax. In addition, studies have shown that good-quality sleep helps increase brain function.

Yet, many people don't put sleep as a priority. Many counseling clients say, "I'll sleep when I'm dead." One thing I know about sleep from my experience is that your body remembers when you don't have enough rest and will want more. This is why some people go on vacation and sleep the time away.

If you're stuck in the pattern of not sleeping, feeling unsafe, and struggling through the day, you're not alone. I was there also. My brain would not shut off. Then it happened suddenly: this divine wisdom came through: "You can activate and reboot your nervous system to have a healthy sleep routine."

So, the next time you can't sleep, go ahead; I invite you, kick you, challenge you, and dare you to raise your Energy in 30 seconds or less naturally so that you Ignite your nervous system to sleep.

Food Energy

What should I eat? How many times in your life have you asked what I should eat for dinner? What should I eat for lunch? What should I eat for breakfast?

The average American will eat almost 1 ton of food a year. Wow! The Energy of food is not just the nutrition. It's the Energy of how you show up and eat the food. To be clear, I am not a nutritionist. Food is Energy, and we will eat until our last day on this planet, so raising your Energy around eating your breakfast, lunch, dinner, and snacks is genius and Ignites you to have more Energy!

Speak. Shine. Speak. from the SHINE ON! book

"I help Shine care for her wellness by only offering her good food. Yet, I have noticed that when her biscuits get stale, she will not eat them."

Health is the new wealth; at least, that's what I've heard. Raising your Energy and the environment's Energy and infusing the food with positive Energy is powerful. When you create this Energy, the vibration aligns with your ultimate nutrition and health.

I suggest two important habits to my clients and friends: eating without distractions and sitting while eating. Examples of no distractions are no screen time and no TV or phone. Without distractions, you will create nurturing and loving Energy with what you eat. To help your body digest your food better, sit and eat. The body is amazing. I did a study with my Reiki students and asked how many stand up and how many sit down when they eat. Their answers were staggering. Fifty-five percent said they stood most of the time, 40% said they sat down, and 5% said they never stop; they eat on the run.

Eliminate mealtime distractions, and your Energy will rise in 30 seconds or less naturally. So, I dare you to take 10 minutes to sit and entirely focus on the food you are eating and know and feel that it is healthy and nurturing your body.

Exercise Energy

> **"Exercise is personal power in action."**
> **~ Angel Marie**

Do you exercise daily? Do you like to exercise? Do you put exercise as a priority? Do you have excuses for not moving your body?

Some excuses I hear from my counseling clients include: it's too hot outside, I don't feel comfortable going to a gym, I don't have time, and I am too busy. Interestingly, research shows that less than 30% of the population moves daily. This is shocking because the obesity rate is so high in the United States alone. Yet, many people are not inspired to take action to move. Research shows that people who exercise regularly live longer, live healthier, and have better brain function and mental health.

During a Tai Chi class, a student told me he had challenges and felt like he was in an emotional pit, overcome with stress, and didn't like his body. However, after just a few sessions, he improved his attitude and felt more motivated to exercise because of the healing Energy of Tai Chi. He was elated because he found a new version of himself and now appreciates his body. Everything is movement; Energy is movement. That's why, even with my crushed big toe, I practice the art of Tai Chi and walk every day. I understand that movement Ignites the nervous system and boosts the immune system. So, being diagnosed with lupus, fibromyalgia, arthritis, and Sjögren's, all immune system diseases, exercise is a priority in my life.

Action Step from the SHINE ON! Book

Breathe... If you are seated, set a timer for one hour. When the timer goes off, get up and move for at least ten minutes. This is not the time to get on the phone or check social media. And breathe…

I challenge you to schedule movement every day, even if it's as simple as getting up and shaking your body for 30 seconds or less. I call this the Shine On Shake. Raise your Energy in 30 seconds or less naturally by getting up and moving.

Morning and Evening Routine Energy

Do you believe that a routine can help you increase your Energy? Do you feel stuck in a rut and suffering through the day? Do you have a morning routine? Do you have an evening routine?

Studies show that the average person in America has a routine, yet exercise and stretching are a small percentage. Shockingly, checking social media ranked higher in the study. It's encouraging that research also revealed that drinking water is on the rise.

Developing a morning and evening routine is powerful because it will help you stay balanced, have more motivation and Energy throughout the day, and sleep better. Here is one example of what helped many of my counseling clients feel better and have more Energy in the morning. After getting out of bed, either standing or sitting up in a chair, take 3 to 10 diaphragmatic breaths. This will help you balance your brain function.

One of the guests on *Your Time To Shine International Interview Series* had an enlightening experience using an evening routine I suggested for her. She had insomnia, slept only 4 hours a night, and couldn't get her brain to quiet down. However, within days of starting the routine, she slept through the night, had more clarity, and was more productive.

Action Step from the SHINE ON! Book

> Breathe... Before leaving the house in the morning, stop, stand in place, spin around and say, "Shine On!" three times. And breathe...

Raise your Energy in 30 seconds or less naturally by adapting a morning and evening routine!

Smile Energy

Do you smile? Do you feel you have a beautiful smile? Do you smile at others? Do you like your smile?

Studies show that smiling reduces stress, helps heart health, and boosts the immune system. There is powerful Energy in a simple smile for the smiler and the person receiving it. We have neurotransmitters from our heads to our toes. When consciously or subconsciously, you put a smile on your face, your body naturally releases endorphins and helps the body balance the emotions. Isn't the human body amazing!

I have witnessed this in myself and my Reiki students after a severe accident. Focusing on smiling helps to reduce pain in the body. It is scientifically proven that smiles are contagious because the human body is hardwired to mimic the expressions of others.

Some research shows that smiling helps you live longer! So, smiling is also part of the Shine On Pledge because it's a good reminder to keep smiling no matter what happens in your life. Smiling will help you to have inspiration and have better boundaries for making those choices that sometimes are a struggle.

So, I encourage you to smile right now and leave that smile on your face as you read this for at least 30 seconds. Studies show that even a fake smile produces all the energizing emotions and chemicals in your body, which Ignites your brain function and overall wellness.

Action Step from the SHINE ON! Book

Breathe… Before leaving your house, look in the mirror, smile, and say out loud, "I feel awesome today!" And breathe…

So, Shine On, put your smile on, and raise your Energy in 30 seconds or less naturally.

Laughter Energy

Have you ever laughed so hard you almost peed your pants? Does it take a lot to get you to laugh? Do you like your laugh? Could you count on one hand how many times you laugh in a day? Would you like to laugh more?

These are important questions about laughter, because it is physically so powerful and it is chemical free Energy, all natural. The mind, brain can create such seriousness and worry that throughout the day you may only get a little chuckle. My Mama used to say when I was a baby, "I'm going to bottle up your Energy so that I can have more." Even today I get asked, "How do you have so much Energy, Angel?" "Laugh, laugh, laugh!"

"I love to laugh. Even a fake laugh can make your body feel good. Try it!" ~ Angel Marie

Don't just try it, do it NOW! Yes, I am a teacher, counselor, and coach, so I do get bossy! Do it NOW!

Scientific studies prove that even a fake laugh creates those feel-good endorphins in the body. So, laughter boosts the immune system. When I read this study on how many times an adult laughs in a day, I wasn't surprised that it's only 17 times. Yet, children laugh over 300 times a day. Wow! Those are significant numbers, right? Laughter is contagious, and there are not many people who, when they are around me even on virtual meetings, if I start to laugh, they don't start to laugh, or at least smile. There are powerful health benefits to laughing, and that is why it is a part of the Shine On pledge to Ignite your laughter.

Speak. Shine. Speak. from the SHINE ON! book

Even Shine laughs! When she's excited or having a lot of fun, she howls. She cannot hold it in, all that joy! It bubbles out in a nice long howl of laughter. I even have a video on my website of her howling because that makes me laugh.

Memories also will Ignite laughter, so sit back and enjoy a good laugh! It will give you more Energy which helps Ignite your creativity, confidence, and abundance.

Laughter is an awesome way to raise your Energy in 30 seconds or less naturally!

Action Step from the SHINE ON! book

Breathe... Take time every morning to look in the mirror and make yourself laugh at least three times. Start with a giggle and work up to a full belly laugh! And breathe...

Hug Energy

Have you had a hug today? Do you like hugs? Do you hug yourself? Do you hug your pet? Hugs are a universal way to greet someone. Touch is an essential part of nurturing your body and raising your Energy!

Studies show that 8 to 12 hugs a day help nurture and open the body's neural pathways, which helps with clarity, confidence, and joy. Heart-to-heart hugs have proven to have more healing Energy. When you're feeling lonely or isolated, hugs instantly boost oxytocin levels. I have seen a hug completely shift anger to acceptance.

When hugging my Reiki students, I hold the hug for at least 10 seconds, with no patting on the back, no moving, just standing and hugging. I tell them, "I am your Reiki Master, yet it's not just me hugging you. The Higher Self/God/Universe is hugging you, too!" So, breathe and relax, and allow your immune system to release any Energy that does not serve you. Also, allow yourself to receive the limitless energizing of every white blood cell that will keep you healthy and disease free.

When hugging someone, I caution you about holding on too long. Let the other person set the tone and length of time of the hug. It is never wise to push a hug on anyone. If you get a limp or a kind of side hug, it's okay. It's not easy to feel safe when getting a hug if you've gone through sexual abuse, as I have, and 4 out of 10 people have been sexually abused.

Go ahead and allow love to flow through your heart by hugging one another. At Shine On Saturdays, I always look forward to Vinny's hugs. I relax into him. He is one of my Reiki Masters and a friend for over 15 years. He has always been safe, loving, and honorable to me. Do you have someone in your life you feel so safe with that when they hold you, you can be okay with it?

Here is a quick way to release Energy: being empathic, highly attuned to my nervous system, and deeply feel Energy, when I meet someone, I approach them with open arms to hug them and hold on as long as they do. Then, when we step back, I clap my hands to release the Energy of that person and clear mine. This simple act helps me Ignite more Energy. So, make it a commitment to get at least 12 hugs a day, and you will boost your Energy in 30 seconds or less naturally and be full of life and joy.

Near Death Heart Attack Story

Have you ever felt so lethargic that you could hardly move, yet you just kept going and wouldn't stop and collapsed when you did? Well, then, you know what I'm talking about. When I owned the Lightworkers Gifts wellness center, I never realized how sick I was until I stopped. I worked six days a week and was blessed with all the volunteers and Reiki students who graciously stepped up to help.

I was getting more depleted and sicker every day and finally went reluctantly to a healthcare provider who said to me, "You are on the verge of a heart attack." I remember looking at him and saying, "Am I going to die?" "You have lupus, fibromyalgia, arthritis, and Sjögren's. Your metabolism runs like a triathlete, and you're working 16-hour days, so I would say yes, definitely a concern. So, what are you doing?" he asked. I told him I had a wellness center, and I was helping people balance their life and teaching them how to heal with Energy, and he said, "*You* have to find a balance. The body can only do so much."

I found myself in this fog. It was like 114° that day when I got into my car, and I was baking, yet all I could do was stare out the front window. I knew I wasn't grounded and stopped, took a deep breath, and started shaking my whole body, and oh my gosh: I then felt grounded to drive. After crying and crying, reviewing my life, and writing for hours, I went back to studying the power of Energy, the power of Nutrition, and the power of Mindset. The magic of combining Energy, nutrition, and mindset helped me regain my health, have a successful counseling, speaking, and Reiki practice, and now I speak globally with people worldwide.

I challenge you to put *your* health first and give yourself permission to put *yourself* first.

Chapter 2 Spirituality Energy

Has this ever happened to you? You drop a glass on a tile floor right before you walk out the door? Or you spill coffee on your shirt? You have everything ready for a speaking engagement, and then you cannot find your outline?

"Spirituality is the unique understanding that there is something in the universe that is greater than yourself."
~Angel Marie

Do you feel that everything happens for a reason? Do you feel that sometimes things just happen, and they just are?

This is important. Consider this: you are driving down the road when you see a tire shop, and this Energy comes through your head that says, "Wow, I haven't had a flat tire in a long time," and then you immediately say, "no, no, cancel and delete don't think of that." Then, later on in the day, you're driving, and you hit a pothole, and you get a flat tire. So, here's the puzzling question, did you create the flat tire, or did you see it before it happened?

Because you were late due to the glass falling on the floor or having to change your shirt because you spilled coffee on it, you hear that you missed an accident that you would have been right in the middle of. Although you may have forgotten your keynote speaker outline, in the end you totally crushed it and the audience loved you. So again, the question: did you see it before it happened, or did you create it?

Studies show that more than half the population feels clumsy or awkward. As a result, they feel ashamed of their actions and frustrated with themselves. Perceiving your actions and connecting to your body Ignites your ability to change the outcome.

Yet, in all my decades of experience, it seems that sometimes life happens! With that being said, every instant of life is an adventure.

By connecting and following your Energy through your body and raising your Energy in 30 seconds or less naturally, you can be more centered and focused.

Meditation Energy

"Meditation is a practice to achieve peace and harmony in your life." ~Angel Marie

Do you practice meditation? Do you pray? Do you have a breathing routine? Have you ever said, "I don't have time to stop and breathe, let alone meditate?" Do you feel judged when people find out you meditate?

Studies show that when you relax the nervous system and meditate, you reduce your stress levels and have more balance and creativity. Meditation outside in nature is one of the most natural ways to shift your DNA. It helps you release negative Energy and achieve higher consciousness so that you are ignited with positive Energy.

When you are in a relaxed state or a meditation Energy field, your body is jumping for joy because that's when it can start rejuvenating and healing itself naturally.

The most common remark about meditation or breathwork I've heard in over two decades of teaching and counseling is, "I tried to meditate, and there were too many voices in my head, I couldn't relax, so I quit trying." Yes, I even said that when I started quieting my mind, too.

At retreats I recommend participants practice meditation 3 to 4 times throughout the day. After the morning routine, pick a time in your schedule to stop from 5 minutes to 15 minutes, lie down and breathe. Diaphragmatic breathing is a great way to start any meditation or return to calm anytime you need to. First, inhale through your nose for 6 seconds, feeling your abdomen expand. Next, hold your breath for 2 seconds. Then, exhale slowly and steadily through your mouth for 8 seconds.

Action Step from the SHINE ON Book

Breathe… Take ten minutes every day to meditate or pray about the core values of your religious or spiritual belief system. Then, write down three ways your spiritual or religious values influence your daily choices. And breathe…

Raising your Energy by focusing on your breathing and relaxing the nervous system helps you to Ignite your Energy and a fresh new look at your life. So, raise your Energy with meditation throughout the day and make it a priority so that you have more creativity and inspiration.

What is a Lightworker?

Lightworker is a made-up word combining the idea of bringing light to the world with a particular technique. However, there seems to be a common understanding that Lightworkers have a passion and mission to make the world brighter. People labeled "Lightworkers" tend to be Empaths, Reiki Healers, Intuitive, Tai Chi Instructors, Spiritual Counselors, and so on. The fact is we are all Lightworkers. If you have compassion and love, you want the world to be a better place, you Shine your light no matter what you're doing.

You could be a grocery store greeter who shares a smile and a kind word. You could be the person who cheers on their friends. You could be using words as a writer to Ignite others. No matter HOW you show up in the world if you're leading with love and kindness, YOU are a Lightworker!

So, here's the bottom line: YOUR Energy is in the collective, and I invite you to be the authentic YOU that you are. Do it YOUR way. Be YOU. Ignite and share YOUR unique light and Shine On!

Reiki Energy Healing

Did you ever want to get a massage? Have you ever heard of Energy healing? Have you ever had a Reiki Energy Healing session? Are you wondering what Reiki is? Have you ever asked yourself, "How do you become a Reiki practitioner?"

Studies have shown Reiki Energy Healing is one of the fastest-growing alternative healing modalities. Rei means universal. Ki means the vital life force Energy. So, Reiki is Universal Life Force Energy, and it applies to all purposes, conditions, and situations. A recent study showed that getting a Reiki session once a week over 8 weeks was more effective than a placebo and reduced anxiety and depression by half, while improving self-esteem. The biggest finding was that Reiki Energy Healing helped the overall quality of life!

Reiki Energy Healing is a form of Energy therapy in which the practitioner, with or without light touch, ignites your natural ability to heal yourself, reduce inflammation, and relieve pain and stress. When you learn about Reiki Energy Healing you will be able to raise your Energy in 30 seconds or less naturally.

Angel Marie's Personal Reiki Story

Have you ever wondered how someone is "called" to be a Lightworker? I always find the stories and journeys interesting because no two are alike. So, I'd like to share mine to give you context for your Energetic journey.

As children, we're often conduits of pure and positive Energy. My journey began as a child. I just loved to bring people together, make them laugh, and spread a little sunshine so that they would feel good because it made me feel good. My Mama would say, "Your Energy is contagious, little one!" and "You light up a room!"

Over 40 years ago, I was diagnosed with lupus, fibromyalgia, arthritis, and Sjögren's syndrome. Add in life experiences that created low self-esteem, no self-worth, and simply not feeling good enough to fit in; I suffered from sleepless nights, sluggish Energy, and chronic pain.

With these diseases, you can only treat the symptoms. And we all know what the medical community will suggest - drugs. That didn't work for me. I looked EVERYWHERE for relief from the constant pain.

While getting my weekly massage, my therapist had to stop touching me because the pain was excruciating. So, she suggested Reiki Energy Healing. After learning that it was about using Energy to heal, coming from a Catholic and Christian background my first response was, "What is it? You can't heal!" Yet, I said, "Okay. Let's try it!"

Within moments, BAM! I felt Energy waves moving and could move the pain Energy out of my body to be pain-free! With that, I learned that I HAD to put self-care as a top priority for myself — from my mindset to my heartset to my gutset (if that's even a word).

Because of this experience, I decided to learn everything I could about this "Energy Healing business," not only for myself; I wanted to share this powerful healing with others. So I was, and am still today, driven to share all I know to offer healing to the world and the tools of self-healing and self-care to as many people as possible.

I searched for a Reiki Master/Teacher and found one who was holding a group class and received my Level 1 attunement. At the time, I did not know that I was an empath and highly intuitive, so I was strongly affected by the Energy of the others in the class, which got in the way of learning the art of Reiki Energy Healing.

So, I repeated my Level 1 training one-on-one with a different Reiki Master. This one-on-one training was so impactful that I continued learning through Level 2 and Master training, to become a Certified Reiki Master. Empowered with this certification, I opened Lightworkers Gifts Energy Healing Center in Phoenix in 2005 to teach and serve others with this holistic approach to wellness.

I feel blessed to have gained this valuable awareness and reconnected to my true happiness! Reiki Energy Healing also brought me back to joy, laughter, and freedom to become the person I was always meant to be: more energetic, more confident, more abundant, and more joyful.

To become a practitioner, you must have a Reiki Master/Teacher give you the training and attunements.

I believe that Reiki heals your systems and organs down to your cells, and I am living proof that Reiki Energy heals the body.

Nature Energy

Would you say you're a nature lover? Are you a tree hugger? Do you go outside at least once a day?

Nature inspires a sense of awe that helps expand our thinking and imagination. Nature also allows us to look at our lives from a different perspective. It often helps us be more creative and boosts our brain functions with increased Energy.

Some studies suggest that at least 2 hours a week of being in the beautiful outdoors helps to increase well-being. My Reiki students have reported that nature is a wonderful antidote for stress, helps to reduce nervous system arousal, and enhances immune system function.

It is also a necessary part of connecting to the energies of healing. Taking your shoes off and feeling Mother Earth's Energy is not only grounding, it also helps heal the body. This is called "Earthing", and many studies have shown that the benefits are diminished chronic pain, increased Energy levels, and even helps you sleep.

So many health benefits; I invite you to prioritize going outside at least 20 minutes a day. Nurture yourself today and increase your Energy naturally within 30 seconds or less just by going outside and taking in the awe of nature.

Spiritual Grounding and Protection Story

I had the honor of facilitating a Full Moon ceremony at the Lightworkers Gifts Energy Healing Center. We had a healing meditation, and at the end of the meditation, there was a beautiful woman who was so deep in meditation that she was not coming back with everyone else. I was saying to everyone, "start moving, start stretching, open your eyes gently when you're ready."

Everyone was moving except for her. I knew immediately that she wasn't sleeping and had gone deep into the healing. I had everyone start breathing and humming, which created a grounding vibrational Energy, and I gently started saying, "It's time to come back. You are safe to come back."

Afterward, she said, "I heard what you were saying, yet I felt so heavy, I didn't want to come back. It felt so wonderful to be in the healing Energy that I was in. Thank you, Angel. I've never felt so safe, comforted, and out of pain. Thank you for the experience."

I have heard this a thousand times, over all of my decades, of people wanting to stay in a place that is so peaceful, beautiful, and timeless.

One of my Reiki students came to me later and said, "Seeing what just happened, I understood why you teach us to make sure we're grounded, and we put protection around ourselves." Another student said, "I understand now that I must have discernment when choosing a facilitator. Because holding the space and making sure that everyone is grounded is being a responsible facilitator. I was so honored by my students and what they learned, which helped me appreciate all these years of teaching Energy Healing.

Visualization Energy

Does visualization take a lot of my time? Is daydreaming a waste of time? Do you have to write down your desires, wants, and needs? Have you ever said, "I was just thinking about a person, and BAM, they called me?"

Does visualization or spending time in a daydream about what you desire work for manifesting your ideal life? I would say Yes!

Research shows that successful CEOs and visionaries spend time daily in the Energy of dreaming the big dream, creating in their mind the pictures and stories of their desires with inspiration and joy. I believe they understand how Energy flows and agree with these concepts. "What you think about, you bring about." "Where your attention goes, your Energy flows." You have heard these before, and if not, take a moment to be present with the concept of your thoughts. I have been teaching and counseling this for years, and it's an important part of the morning and evening routines I teach.

My ultimate daydream desire was to certify a Reiki Master in Maui, Hawaii, which came true because of the daily practice of visualization. Just minutes a day of breathing, writing, seeing, feeling, and believing I am on top of the mountain at Haleakala, above the clouds. What a dream, and then, BAM! It happened!

My student called and said, "I am ready to go to Master Level," and all the arrangements fell into place with great ease and grace. I was gifted with the trip of my dreams to Hawaii for no cost! I felt so honored to have a sacred Reiki Attunement ceremony on top of the mountain, and the Energy was so powerful it felt smooth and calming. I was not surprised that my dream, my vision, came true. However, I was astonished that I was speechless and so calm. Remember, just because you can't see it doesn't mean it's not there or not going to happen.

A proven way to Ignite your visualization skills is with breathing. Design a manifestation poster. Attach pictures or words of your desires. Put it on the ceiling above your bed or on the refrigerator. While staring at it, visualize your dreams and tell the story. Raise your Energy in 30 seconds or less naturally by daydreaming.

Tai Chi Energy

Have you ever heard of Tai Chi? Has your doctor suggested that you should go outside and practice Tai Chi? Have you seen people early in the morning at parks having fun flowing with Tai Chi? Have you wondered if this slow-moving exercise really helps your health? Practicing Tai Chi can reboot your body naturally and help you to feel more alive.

Research shows that practicing Tai Chi can help with muscle strength, flexibility, and balance.

Many of my Tai Chi students find that it helps with balance, increases Energy, and they feel a sense of value and purpose.

My healthcare advisor told me over a decade ago, "Start practicing Tai Chi, which will help you with your stress because you are on the verge of a heart attack. You need to slow down." I remember hearing those words and thinking, "Oh my gosh, am I going to die? Slow down, me? Wow! That will be interesting to see and feel!"

Yet, when I started practicing the beautiful art of Tai Chi every week at Lightworkers Gifts, I fell in love with the rhythm of the dance. Truth be known, I sat for many months of the class while working to build core muscles. Finally, after 90 days, I could stand and flow with my whole body! Once I felt better, I studied and received my certification to teach. That was over a decade ago.

The art of Tai Chi embodies the yin and yang concept on multiple levels. First, it helps integrate body and mind with movements that create rhythmic Energy, conscious breathing, and heightened self-awareness.

Second, I found that when your Energy is blocked, your brain function can decrease, and disease can appear in the body.

Practicing Tai Chi 2 times a day is powerful. Having morning and evening routines and including Tai Chi helps Ignite your Energy and improves your mental health. Even though Tai Chi is a slow movement, and many may feel it is not really exercising, science shows Tai Chi can improve overall health. When you Ignite your Chi (Energy), you Ignite your power. Surprise me on a Saturday morning at the park, let's do the dance...

Get your flow of Chi moving through the body, and in 30 seconds or less, you will raise your Energy and feel better naturally.

Intuitive Reading Energy

Have you ever had a tarot or palm reading? How about an aura or angel card reading? Have you sat with a psychic and asked questions about your life?

Research shows that Psychic services are on the rise and will continue to increase with the uncertainty of the world. There are many spiritually gifted people who give amazing insights. Every single reading can be eye-opening, a great source of healing, and help you see beliefs in a different way.

It's important to note that every reading you get will be different because your Energy field vibrates differently each time. The same is true for the Reader because their Energy fields are different and their interpretation of you, your Energy, and the cards are different, too. So as a reminder, do your research and use discernment when looking for a Reader, Medium or Psychic.

Getting a reading can be fun and exciting! A reading can Ignite your perception of your life and shift it to an all-new level. It has been my absolute pleasure to deliver messages of hope and inspiration for over 2 decades.

Getting a reading could Ignite your ability to raise your Energy in 30 seconds or less naturally.

Crystal Energy

Do you have any crystals? Have you always wondered what's the big deal about crystals? Have you ever said I don't feel anything when I touch a crystal? Do you think crystals are "woo woo"?

Whether you feel the Energy or not, everything is Energy, and we all are vibrating and can connect to Energy outside of ourselves.

Studies have shown that different types of crystals have different vibrational fields. Even a rock has a vibrational Energy field. Did you know that Google searches for Crystal healing have more than doubled in the past 5 years? This is because of the mainstream and science revealing the healing properties of crystals. Your body's Energy is a conductor and activates crystals that can heal the body.

I have found that the majority of the population does not understand crystals nor believe that they're important in their life. The studies that I've done with countless people show that learning about your Energy field vibration helps to tap into other energies, including crystals. This is why some people can feel crystal Energy and others do not.

There are many books, apps that will give you the meaning and definition of a crystal. In my experience of teaching crystal classes for over 20 years, people expect to feel the feeling described in the book instead of the actual vibration of the crystal.

Example: If you believe an amethyst crystal will help with addiction and you hold the crystal and have the belief it's going to help you not to drink or not to take drugs, your emotions will take over and you won't indulge in your addiction, because you believe that the crystal will help you get through it.

I enjoy helping others experience crystals in my classes and using crystals in healing sessions and crystal layouts. Crystal layout sessions are powerful, and my clients have had amazing results because they were ready and open to heal...

Was it the crystal that healed, or was it their belief? This is a question that has been asked for years, yet there are so many personal stories about how crystals healed whatever ailed the person. So, I invite you to explore crystals because they can Ignite your ability to heal yourself and help you to raise your Energy in 30 seconds or less naturally.

Complete Electricity Outage Story

It was a cool summer day at 111° outside. I woke up at my normal time - way early, went downstairs, opened the fridge, and noticed the fridge light was dim. I thought, "How did the light bulb get dim in the refrigerator? That's a new one on me."

So, of course, I reached out and asked for help and called my dad. Dad was an electrician. He came over immediately since he lived up the street. He opened the refrigerator and looked at me, puzzled, in a Daddy Bear way. I remember thinking, "Oh, s***! Here it comes."

Outside, at the circuit box, Dad said, "You fried the main Energy line coming into your condo. I've only heard of this a couple of times." My first reaction was, "Oh my gosh! Mama was right; I am Special."

Back in the house, the light bulbs started going off and on. Then suddenly, I remembered, "Oh my gosh, I left the computers on," and I ran upstairs just as the computers went down.

Fast forward: Utility serviceperson showed up and confirmed Dad's assessment. When he looked at the box, he said, "Yes, the whole main line is gone." He gave me a puzzled look. Then he looked at my car and saw the words Lightworkers Gifts Energy Healing. He said, "You're a Lightworker?" I was amazed. "Yes, I am," I said. "I've seen this happen before," he said. "I fried my main electricity coming to my condo?" I asked. "Yes!" he said. "Energy is Energy," I said.

I took the study of quantum physics to a higher level of understanding of how Energy flows, gets stuck, shifts, changes, and heals. You know you are powerful, and you could fry your electricity also.

Chapter 3 Mundane Tasks Energy

Do you get bored when it comes to the humdrum activities of your life? Are you lacking the Energy to do the dishes, clean the house or do the shopping?

"Exercise your playful spirit and Shine On!"
~ Angel Marie

Grooming Energy

Have you ever felt like, what's the point? I just did this yesterday, or this morning. Why do I need to take a shower, brush my hair, or brush my teeth?

Studies say the average American spends more than 3/4 of their life grooming and cleaning themselves. It might come with a fight or mental argument in their heads. Tell me if you can relate. They sound like this: "get up, go take a shower, no sit here a little longer, no, no wait, go take a shower? You could use a manicure today. Forget it, just do it tomorrow."

We must keep in mind that grooming, keeping ourselves clean, and taking care of our health will be a personal chore until the moment we leave this planet. Yet, if you choose not to do it someone else will end up grooming, cleaning, and nurturing your body.

Taking better care of your outer appearance starts with loving the person you see in the mirror. Giving yourself permission to put yourself first is a way to increase your power and feel better about yourself.

Loving the person you see in the mirror will raise your Energy, get you off the couch, and stop you from arguing with yourself. Raising your Energy will begin to change the language you speak with yourself. The gentle, loving whisper will start to raise your Energy naturally, and within 30 seconds or less, it will Ignite you to get your butt moving. This activity of taking care of our appearance will improve your health and put a smile on your face.

Shower Energy

Have you ever said, "I don't want to go take a shower I don't have the Energy for that? What does it matter if I take a shower? I'm not going anywhere today! I don't like taking a shower, it's boring."

Did you know that studies say that the average person spends more than 60 hours a year in the shower? Taking a shower before you go to sleep will reduce stress and help you sleep better. So, let's make taking a shower a fun experience and one that raises your Energy.

Showers are a great time to rinse off negative Energy and boost your Energy naturally. Also, showering helps the nervous system relax and increases blood circulation.

Every body part has a different Energy field, and when you are taking a shower, if you speak to the different body parts it will boost healing. Saying, "I love you elbow and thank you," while you are touching your elbow is powerful. You are raising the Energy of the whole body, which will help reduce body pain.

It's just like singing and raising the Energy of your food. You are putting positive Energy into the food and also boosting the appreciation of the food. By accepting and acknowledging your body parts in this way you start to accept your body on a subconscious level which helps you be more present and healing in the moment. This is very fundamental for your self-image and overall body image.

Action Step from the SHINE ON! book

Breathe... Every day in the shower, sing, "I am happy! I share happy! Happy feels great! I love happy!" Say it. Sing it. Write it. And breathe...

So, enjoy the benefits of a healing shower and raise your Energy naturally today.

Cleaning Dishes Energy

Do you feel like the dishes just keep piling up? Are you lacking the Energy or inspiration to take action to clean the dishes? This is a commonality with every person I know. Sooner or later, you're going to have to clean a dish.

Did you know that the average American will do dishes for 25 minutes a day? Let's take this mundane task and boost our Energy to have more enthusiasm to get the dishes done. The research I did with my Tai Chi group showed that putting a mirror up in front of the sink helped raise their Energy with their smiles!

Fun tip: I learned along the way to get a workout and raise the Energy while doing the dishes. Open the cabinets underneath the sink so that you can bend your knees into the cabinet, lean on the sink, and create a position as in Tai Chi. Then start to sway back and forth and, as you look in the mirror, smile and do the dishes! Your position and your smile will Ignite your enthusiasm for washing dishes! Go ahead and try it today. Okay, trying is lying, so just do it!

Raise your Energy in 30 seconds or less naturally by doing the dishes.

Laundry Energy

Do you like doing laundry? Do you have piles of laundry waiting for you? Do you ever do half the laundry and then leave the pile of clean clothes waiting to put them away? Do you do laundry every day?

Let's be real here, laundry can be dull and mundane. Studies show that the average person will spend 63 hours a year doing laundry. Also, the average household does about 10 to 15 loads of laundry a month. Did you know that 70% of dirt on clothes is invisible, and it's actually human matter like dead skin cells, sweat, and natural body oils? That's gross, so let's do some laundry!

Laundry Energy is a form of self-care and can be a very calming and gratifying activity. Yet many times, repetitive tasks tend to become a tedious activity. This is how I have fun and practice Tai Chi and create a whole new dance.

Imagine breathing and stretching while you are putting the laundry in the washer, into the dryer, folding the clothes, putting them away, and consciously breathing through each step. You will raise your Energy and feel awesome! Be in grateful gratitude for your body, the laundry, your Higher Self/God/Universe, and the money that gave you the means to have all of this. Always reward yourself for completing the laundry and celebrate the workout!

Raise your Energy in 30 seconds or less naturally by working out and getting your laundry done.

House Cleaning Energy

Do you get excited about cleaning your house? Do you like to vacuum? Do you schedule house cleaning, vacuuming, dusting, cleaning the bathroom, changing your sheets?

Studies show that the average person will clean their home for 6 hours a week. Getting inspired to clean and release the old Energy will raise the Energy in your home. Further research shows that you can feel the excitement of cleansing and clearing all vibrational fields around your material items with gratitude and appreciation.

Life is going to happen, no matter whether you participate or not, yet your Energy matters, and this physical body and your environment absolutely affect the emotions and Energy sources in your body. Think about it: when you do not vacuum for weeks, take a shower for days, change your sheets, dust the house, or clean the bathrooms, all of that dirt and dead skin adds up. This creates a lower vibrational field in your home and in your personal Energy field.

You probably have beautiful figurines, crystals, and art pieces you have collected along your life path. Many of these items bring you joy and remind you of happy memories. All of these collectibles hold Energy. Studies about collecting knick-knacks and material items are astonishing. Collecting is a human instinct.

When I was a kid, Saturday morning cleaning the house was so much fun with my Mama. Music would be cranked, the whole house would be open, and the family was cleaning and singing happily, knowing that we were bringing in positive Energy and raising the frequency. When we were done, I got to go outside and play all day.

Put on some music, and I'm not talking about meditation music. I'm talking rock and roll, hip hop, something that gets you moving. As a matter of fact, stop what you are doing right now, grab your cell phone and say, "Pandora or Spotify play 'Shine On' by Angel Marie!" Hehe, that will get you going!

Using the dust cloth to clean off the old Energy helps boost the Energy of the memories of the items. Raise your Energy in 30 seconds or less naturally by getting excited to pick up each piece and energize it. This will cleanse and clear it and then amplify it with gratitude and joy. Dusting in this way creates positive Energy and inspires you to dust even more often. The memories of the items can help you reignite the joy and fun of collecting them.

Schedule house cleaning on your calendar today to manifest your desires and open the Energy fields to flow with more confidence, joy, and abundance.

Raise your Energy in 30 seconds or less naturally by cleaning today for more abundance in your life!

Decluttering Energy

Are you living with clutter? Does clutter give you anxiety? Would you like to get rid of clutter? Do you lack boundaries when it comes to clutter?

Research shows that getting rid of excess stuff can benefit your mental health by making you feel calmer, happier, and more in control. Studies also show that people with cluttered homes tend to suffer from insomnia and are more likely to be overwhelmed.

Energy cannot flow through a space with boxes and clutter.

This visual stimulant of excessive Energy in stuff signals to the brain that our work is never done, and also creates Energy of guilt, anxiety and feelings of being overwhelmed. Remember a cluttered environment creates a cluttered mind.

The first thing is to view your home as a first-time visitor and make a list of what you want to declutter. One way to get yourself inspired is to schedule decluttering and start with 15 minutes and then work up to one hour every day. Do it now! Clear up the space and relax the mind by reducing the clutter.

When clutter is present you may feel stuck in your social life as well as your relationship with others and yourself. Think about it: decluttering will help you Ignite your Energy so that you can have better loving relationships. Being able to recharge in a peaceful calm home is powerful and science even suggests that clutter causes unforeseen health issues. Raise your Energy in 30 seconds or less naturally and take action to get decluttered today!

Shopping Energy

Do you like to go shopping? Do you prefer online shopping or in person shopping? Is shopping retail therapy for you? Do you get stressed out when you have to go shopping? Do you struggle to find the item you're looking for?

Studies show that more than 80% of shopping is done by women. Studies also show that the leading source of debt is excessive credit card spending due to impulse buying by both men and women.

More than one of my counseling clients has told me that their overspending is due to feeling, "I deserve that and want it now." Over 75% of the population orders online at least once a month. With the rise of online shopping, self-sabotaging behavior is contributing to financial debt and increased anxiety. So next time you find yourself shopping, take a moment to create a pattern interrupt by walking away from the computer, or ask yourself, "Do I really need this item?"

One of my Reiki students asked me, "Why do I feel so much anxiety when I go clothes shopping?" I told her that, many times, people compare themselves to an unrealistic ideal of how they want to look in clothes. Appreciating your body type and expressing gratitude that you can go shopping for yourself will raise your Energy.

Every item in a store has Energy from other people, most of the time it is a lower vibration. Before you go to a store clear your Energy, ground your Energy, and create a positive Energy field around you so that you can make better choices and find things more easily. In this way you will Ignite self-confidence and have a better self-image.

Raise your Energy in 30 seconds less naturally to gain clarity in all your shopping adventures.

Chapter 4 Relationship Energy

Energy is like an invisible thread that holds people together and allows connections to be formed and lasting bonds created. Whether it's romantic or professional or within your family, the Energy exchanged is what will determine the depth and length of that relationship. This Energetic pull is the foundation of the Law of Attraction, "like attracts like". This simply means things with similar Energy levels are drawn to each other. That is, two people vibrating at the same frequencies are pulled towards each other.

> **"Create clarity in all your communications**
> **and you will Shine On!"**
> **~ Angel Marie**

Self-Relationship Energy

Are you aware of your relationship with yourself? Are you your own best friend? Do you know how to put yourself first?

Our relationships are multifaceted from relationships with politics, sex, family, and pets. There are many different kinds of relationships, and yet the most powerful and nurturing relationship is the one you have with yourselves.

Studies show that more than half the population lacks a relationship with themself. More than half lack the connection to self and really understanding who they are.

The Ignite Your Life 90-day Reboot Program teaches people how to connect with themselves, and they learn how to put their relationship with themselves first, before others, society, or fame. The ultimate relationship with self is giving yourself permission to put yourself first. It means self-acceptance and taking the time to nurture yourself and boost your Energy naturally. One way to put yourself first is put your own name in your schedule and consistently take time for yourself.

The most powerful relationship with self is the Energy of acceptance. Acceptance and inspired action boost your Energy naturally to Ignite your self-image and soar to greater heights. It shifts you to the level of knowing your own power and loving yourself. A great way to do this is every time you look in the mirror smile and say, "I accept myself exactly the way I am."

I always express to everyone that they matter. Their Energy helps others, so they can serve others by serving themselves by staying connected to self.

Raise your Energy in 30 seconds or less naturally with a smile and putting yourself first.

Friendship Energy

Do you have a good friend? Do you have a group of trusted friends? Would you consider yourself a good friend?

Studies show that friendship helps you keep your brain function high and your body in shape. Research also proves friendship improves your sleep and can help counteract stress and anxiety. Another study showed that the average person has 3 to 5 good friends in their lifetime, and that many adults don't have very many friends or none at all.

With this being said, creating that deep, engaging exchange with another person instead of surface level conversations takes time and Energy. It may be challenging for you to get out and meet new people. Yet, the rewards are limitless!

To be a good friend and to have friends is a blessing and a gift. So many of my counseling clients have said, "Now that I am older, I don't have as many friends and it's harder to make friends." They also say, "I want to have more friends yet I'm not sure I want to put in the Energy to start a new friendship." I get that with life being busy, taking the time and trusting someone else can be challenging. So, when starting a new friendship, a good practice is to identify what kind of friendship you want with the other person and how you are going to show up. The key to this is communicating it to your new friend. A big part of being a friend is being vulnerable and letting the other person in. Having strong boundaries and communicating these boundaries helps in all relationships.

A good friend is one who asks how you're doing, wants to hang out, and always shows up when the rest of the world walks out. This Energy of friendship takes time to cultivate and starts with you. Being your own best friend with good boundaries and goals helps Ignite the Energy to create a framework for a wonderful relationship.

One of the benefits of a good friendship is being able to raise your Energy naturally just by a conversation. Also, allowing yourself to feel appreciation and acceptance is the gift you give yourself. It's never too late to make a new friend.

Raise your Energy in 30 seconds or less naturally by calling a good friend today!

Action Step from the SHINE ON! book

> Breathe... Once a week, sit with a trusted friend, coach, or family member. Brainstorm one idea to better understand your passion. Write one action to perform each week. And breathe...

Near Death Cliff Jumping Story

Have you ever jumped off a cliff into a lake? Does cliff-jumping sound like fun to you?

Ever since I was 6 years old living here in Phoenix, AZ, we have always gone on camping and lake trips. When I was in college, I had beautiful friends who all had boats and jet skis, so I did my share of jumping off cliffs. I loved the feeling of the adrenaline rush. Many people say, "You're crazy, Angel!" and I say, "Where's the next cliff? Let's do it!"

For the day of my birth, I always create a special event. For my 58th birthday, I asked my dear friend and Reiki Master Victor and his fiancé to join me at the lake to jump off the

30-foot cliff. It was a beautiful sunny 111° day, and we had a wonderful time.

After seeing the pictures and video on social media, Tricia called and said, "I've never jumped off a cliff before. Will you take my husband and me?" It's a treacherous climb to the cliffs. Yet, I said, "Of course! I am so excited to go on an adventure with you and your husband. And I am always up for cliff diving!"

Little did I know that it would end with me stepping out of my comfort zone and into the courage to go off an 80-foot cliff. It was an extraordinary day of waving down jet skiers and getting rides, and basking in the cool Arizona weather of 111°.

As I was floating on the raft in the lake, Tricia yelled, "Angel, let's go up there and jump." I immediately said, "Okay!" It took two high school boys to help us get up the treacherous trail to the 80-foot cliff.

Picture this: we are on top of the mountain and the temperature is still 111°. I'm dehydrated. I can hardly swallow. I'm being fried by the sun, and I'm thinking, "Wait a minute: what am I doing? I did not check in with my Higher Self/God/Universe if this was the wisest choice for me to make."

So reluctantly, I checked in with my Higher Self/God/Universe, and I got a "NO, don't do this," which was a powerful Energy.

I told Tricia, "You go first." She said, "Okay."

Interestingly enough, you can see in the video before she takes off, I have the high school boys help me to get to her to hug her before she goes.

She jumps! Everybody is cheering! Now they're cheering for me, and I'm stuck in emotions of, "Oh my gosh, what do I do now?" I yelled out loud, "I got this, I can do this, I can do this," and I jumped! I'm going through the air for what feels like forever. Halfway down, I think, "Oh my gosh! I'm still falling." The fear Energy was so extreme that I pulled my legs up to protect myself and hit my butt smack on the lake. As my dear best friend Barb Anderson said, "You didn't do a belly flop. You did an A** flop! Heh heh heh."

The impact on my spine caused my legs to go numb, and the pain shooting up to my neck was so severe I had no movement in my legs. I bobbed my head out of the water and screamed, "Tricia!" I could faintly hear her yelling, "Angel, are you okay?" I was going down, not being able to move my legs. Because of the pain I couldn't move my arms. Tricia swam out and rescued me. I said, "Leave me here. I have to relax my body. I am in such pain. I must relax." She helped me to relax while everyone else was running down the mountain to help. I finally got out of the water and asked them to lay me headfirst onto the rock so that Mother Earth could help heal me.

And as they put wet towels on me and poured water, I lay there and took deep diaphragmatic breaths of healing and energetically asked all of my Reiki students to send me healing and strength. My thoughts were, "It takes 3 people on this treacherous mountain to get to the cliffs. How am I going to get back out?" I was in shock!

An hour later, I could barely walk, and we started the treacherous hike back to the car. When we got back to the car, I was shaking so badly that Tricia and her husband rushed to get my food, and I started to relax. I was still in so much pain, and I kept saying, "No blood, no foul, no whining!" I finally asked Tricia to look at my butt to see how bad it was. Just seeing her face told me it was bad, and I said,

"Get me home now!"

When I got home, they set me up to lie on the Reiki table with ice, and I started calling my doctor, chiropractor, nurses, and Reiki students to get advice and help. I teach everyone to ask for help, and I gave myself permission to ask for help. Within hours my students were coming over with food and sharing Reiki Energy Healing. The overwhelming beautiful nurturing and healing I received from so many was eye opening and so loving. I received beautiful dinners, vacuuming of my home, walking Shine, all due to asking for help.

This is important to note because, everything I teach, from my Shine On Song to the SHINE ON! book is always "ask for help," and I was honored to receive help and blessed by the dear souls for the experience.

Here is the lesson learned and received with big Energy: before you decide to do something outside your comfort zone take a moment and ask your Higher Self/God/Universe first!!

This way you may not be on top of a mountain at 111°, dehydrated, and arguing with your Higher Self/God/Universe!

Absolutely jumping off a cliff raises your Energy in 30 seconds or less naturally for sure!

Partnership Energy

Are you with the love of your life? Are you with your soulmate? Are you in love and happy? Can you be yourself around your partner?

Studies show that half the failed marriages in the US fail due to communication issues. Studies also showed that only 53% of those who chose to separate or divorce said they were happy. The commonality with all humans is that we're emotional and we want to feel safe. In a love relationship where there's honesty, acceptance and respect we can face life's challenges with better insights and hope.

It's important to cultivate time being in the present moment with your partner so that you both grow together. Also, creating the Energy of excitement to be with your partner is fun and powerful!

I was asked at a women's event, "Should I stay with my partner? How do I know when to leave?" I took a moment and asked her, "Do you like your partner? Are you staying there because that's what society or religion says you are supposed to do?"

These questions are important questions to ask yourself in any relationship. Many times, you will find that you have grown apart and there is not even a friendship there. It's more of a roommate relationship, and according to studies, this is more common as we age.

Everything, including time, is Energy. When you're wanting to connect to another person, it's the time you spend together is important, not only the activities you do together. Sharing the feeling of joy Energy will help you to grow together. This takes time every single day, so making time for each other is important and should be a priority.

A key element to this is making sure you share the Energy of chores in the house which includes the bills, cleaning, and shopping. Of course, there are always compromises.

For over 20 years of counseling others, one of my biggest tips for any relationship is always remember the little things. Leave a little note that they find in their wallet or send a text that says, "I'm thinking of you." It's the little things that add up to the Energy that creates the excitement and mutual love.

Action Step from the SHINE ON! Book

Breathe... Once a day, have an in-person, face-to-face conversation. Be attentive to gestures, eye contact, and facial expressions. And breathe...

Raise your Energy in 30 seconds or less naturally so that your partner is your favorite treat of the day.

Sex Energy

How do you define sex? Do you enjoy sex? What is the first thing that comes to your mind about sex? Do you feel sex is dirty or should be kept secret? Are you comfortable talking about sex?

Research shows that a healthy sex life helps improve self-esteem, lowers blood pressure, reduces pain and helps with sleep. Sex between two consenting adults is fun and a gift to help boost your immune system and build strength. Studies prove that releasing sexual Energy helps balance the body, improves self-esteem, and decreases depression.

I believe and feel that having sex with yourself, or the act of sex, is positive Energy movement. Yet, in many people are taught that sex is dirty and should be kept secret. I feel that we all have personal freedom of choice and, that by moving sexual Energy you help your body clear unwanted Energy and boost the happy ones. Orgasms are beneficial in igniting Chi (Energy) and manifesting your desires.

This is what I share with each of my Reiki students in a one-on-one Level 1 Reiki training. I start with, "I hope that I do not offend you or make you feel uncomfortable and I know that most Reiki Master/Teachers do not talk about sex, yet I will. Sex is Energy and it's way too powerful not to talk about and use for healing, confidence, and creativity."

In Reiki training I also teach about the Shining Wheel, a medicine wheel. I explain that, in the fire position, sexual Energy is represented. Fire must express itself, flow and burn brightly and freely. Honoring the fire within you, your passion, commitment and purpose in your life is important and vital for your mental wellbeing. So Yes, Yes, every day or every other day give yourself permission to have an orgasm and release negative Energy and create a vibrational Energy field around you that Ignites creativity and joy. Follow your sexual Energy. Passion creates emotion, and the physical touch nurtures your soul and is a healthy way to move your Energy.

Raise your Energy in 30 seconds or less naturally by creating nurturing sex Energy.

Grief Energy

Have you experienced grief? Are you in grief over a passed loved one? Have you ever felt different because of grief? Is grief a way of life for you right now?

Recent studies of what happens in our brains when we experience grief show grieving is a form of learning that teaches us how to be in the world without someone we love. The brain has coded the "we" as much as the "you" and the "I." The brain learns to experience the world differently through grief. You can use grief Energy to Ignite the lessons that life is giving you.

The Energy of grief can be very challenging. You know this yourself because you have experienced a loss of some kind in your life. Whether it be a loved one through death, the end of a friendship or family relationship, or even an opportunity lost. Experiencing this Energy emotionally, physically, and psychologically can be very heavy and can cause restless sleep. Yet here's what I know: You have the power to process loss as quickly or slowly as you need to, or you get to.

Since I work with Energy Healing, people who are challenged with grief Energy, either personally or around them, seek me out, especially the ones who have gone through the loss of suicide.

Because I have experienced it, too, I can counsel them with tools to help them shift their grief to a gift. I provide a safe space for healing with an open heart in order to reboot the mind, body and emotions. I am familiar with this Energy because the love of my life committed suicide soon after we married. I accepted grief and emotionally allowed myself to go through every stage of grief, and I used the power of Energy Healing to help move me through it quickly with grace. This doesn't mean there was not lots of crying.

When you need support in moving through the grief process and transforming the Energy, please reach out. You are not alone. You have the power and tools within you to move through this and be able to move from the breakdown to celebrating the breakthrough with ease, grace, and glory.

"Grief is the gift we release to attain greater happiness."
~ Angel Marie

As you know from 7th-grade science, Energy cannot be created nor destroyed, only converted from one form to another. You do not remove the emotional pain. You transform it to acceptance and joy. Remembering the lost relationships or situations Ignites the moments of what was. Grief triggers are surprising and unpredictable. I get it. Grief doesn't magically disappear. However, you can transform the pain into joy and acceptance by reaching out for support and help.

Raise your Energy in 30 seconds or less naturally to embrace grief.

Action Step from the SHINE ON! Book

> Breathe…Give yourself permission to cry to release your grief. Say out loud, "I release and accept happiness in my life." And breathe…

Elder Care Energy

Are you in the midst of caring for an elder? Is your family starting to talk about who is going to take care of Mom and Dad or Grandma and Grandpa?

Research shows there is a growing number of elders who need care. It is emotional to see a strong vibrant, full-of-life family member confused, angry and depressed.

Here's a way to nurture your Energy and help them in the process. Take time to breathe and center yourself then say out loud," I feel happy, I feel happy!" Keep repeating it until you really feel it. This happy Energy around you will help them to feel happy, yet it will also keep you in the present moment which helps them feel valued and loved. You will have more patience too.

Raising your Energy and staying balanced will help them to feel your Energy of balance and love which is life-changing for them. I have felt this personally with my counseling clients and in my own family. The ability to stay present with your Energy flow of compassion is nurturing to you both.

So, next time you're with an elder get your Happy on and let them set the tone. Be at peace with happy Energy so that you both can feel it. This will Ignite your compassion and enthusiasm for elder care and raise your Energy in 30 seconds or less naturally!

Birthday Energy

Do you celebrate your birthday? Do you like to celebrate others' birthdays? Do you tell everyone it's your birthday and always have a party? Do you like giving or receiving a surprise party? Do you get excited about your birthday?

Studies have shown that more than half of the population don't like their birthdays and feel extreme sadness and anxiety around their birthday. I was surprised by this because imagine being raised in a household that celebrated birthdays with a special dinner, your favorite cake, and always a party. My Mama put Happy Birthday signs everywhere!

I believe that Birthday Energy lasts for three days: from one day prior to your birthday through one day after. It's interesting that the highest vibration is at the moment you came into this existence. Look at your birth certificate for the exact time of your birth.

Many Lightworkers will say that it is this moment in time when you were born that gives you an opportunity to revisit, review, and even rejuvenate what has happened in your life. It's a great time for a vision board and a ceremony of acceptance and manifesting your desires.

Also, I believe that these three days are a powerful time for you to unplug from screen time and get into nature to Ignite, align, and reactivate your DNA. A secret I teach and practice is to do this once a month starting with one half day and increase by baby steps to get to a full day, then three days.

My ultimate birthday surprise party was when I turned 40 and my friends flew in from all over the world for the big celebration. It was the last time I jumped off the roof of a house into a pool. Yet, at 59 years young I jumped off an 80-foot cliff into a lake. But I digress...

Angel's 40th Birthday Story

Little did I know what was going to happen. Picture this: a 6-foot-3-inch drag queen corners me in the kitchen. Before I know it, everyone is around the kitchen, and I'm being roasted by my dear friend the drag queen. With every single story she told I would hold my breath and wait to see how it was going to turn out. It was fun for all, and everything was going smoothly while everybody was playing nicely and leaving out all of the most embarrassing details that would have totally busted me in front of everyone, including my partner and our four-year-old daughter.

Then it happened. The last roast of the night was from a beloved friend who, interesting enough, was not even there. I will never repeat what she said, however, I will always remember how everyone in the room stopped and I was speechless, and my face was so red! I started backpedaling big time, saved by my partner who laughed and laughed, thank goodness!

Birthdays are special and I've always been blessed by wonderful parties, surprise parties, and people who support me and want to celebrate and party with me.

Give yourself permission to be celebrated!! Give your friends the opportunity to celebrate you! So, on your next birthday, have a party, create signs, and put them all over the house. Or you can ask your partner, friends, or family to do it.

Ask for what you want and take time to visualize your desires, create a new vision board, and Ignite the Happy Birthday Energy! Call me on your birthday and I will sing Happy Birthday to you! I dare you to call....

Raise your Energy in 30 seconds or less naturally by celebrating the celebration of life... YOU!!

Pet Energy

Do you have any pets? Are you a cat person or a dog person? Do you like to be around animals?

Studies have found that being around animals can decrease levels of stress and anxiety. Not only that, owning a cat or dog cuts a person's risk of having a stroke or a fatal heart attack by half. In one study, dogs decreased the patients' blood pressure by about 10%.

Pets vary from guinea pigs to dogs, and of course, cows, that in many cultures are revered as pets. Yet, pets can be frustrating, time consuming, and emotionally draining. It's so heartbreaking when it's time for a beloved animal companion to cross over the rainbow bridge.

A Lightworker was so distraught after they lost their pet during the same week their Aunt and a good friend died. They felt ashamed because they had more emotion and sadness over the dog than they did for the Aunt and friend. It is important to note that emotions, no matter how they're expressed, are never right or wrong. It is natural for you to feel the heartbreak. I will give this advice: Grief is never quantified for one person or wrong or right for others. Accepting your grief Energy for your pet will help you heal.

The beauty of pet Energy is that you create your bond with your pet, and they show up with unconditional love and always wanting to please. Pets have an innate ability and an instinct to never give up, to always find a way. Do you feel inspired by your pet? I know I do...

Shine's Story from the SHINE ON! book

My dear friend Lisa Maldonado, Reiki Master and dog trainer, helped me rescue an Australian cattle dog. When I saw Shine, she was shining in the sunlight and the "angel kisses" on her coat lit up my heart. It was love at first sight! As she played in the yard at the animal shelter, I experienced a renewed feeling of freedom and inner joy. I suddenly called out to her by the name "Shine." She heard her new name in my voice and bounded over to me, covering me with kisses. We connected instantly, and my whole world shifted. Since that day, Shine's unconditional love and amazing healing gifts bring joy to all who meet her. Come meet Shine at Shine On Saturdays!

Pets Ignite your Energy naturally by their loving presence. I always recommend to my clients that bonding with a pet is a GIFT. Even a turtle has an Energy field that will Ignite your Energy.

Raise your Energy in 30 seconds or less naturally by being with your pet.

Chapter 5 Work Energy

Do you enjoy your job? Does your job give you a sense of purpose? Are you happy with going to work?

"Embrace your mission to create your amazing life."
~Angel Marie

Work/Job Energy

Are you inspired to get up in the morning and create an impact in your life that fulfills you, plus pays you well? Do you dream of the day where you no longer have to work?

Studies show that over 50% of the people feel emotionally detached at their job and 19% are miserable. Only 33% feel engaged. Most workers view the work they do as "just a job to get them by" rather than a passion in their life.

One of the questions I ask all my guests on the *Your Time to Shine International Interview TV Series* is how do you Ignite and inspire yourself to want to serve others? What is your passion, what do you do that makes you money? Many times, the answer is that they are passionate about helping others or they love their service or believe in their product. Many of my counseling clients have 9 to 5 jobs and have told me that their inspiration comes from enjoying their coworkers and being in alignment with the organization's values and mission.

Many people struggle with what career or job they would like to pursue. Every day is a new day to go on the adventure to practice new opportunities. The journey to Ignite the passion inside of you, the Energy inside of you, can help you feel good about contributing to the human race. When you are fulfilled, you're proud of your work.

When I was in high school, I was a cook at a restaurant. OK, it was at Shakey's Pizza Parlor, and I made pizza. However, in college I was a mechanic in Newport Beach, California. I've also owned a cleaning company and also was co-owner of a coffee cart. I was a softball coach for 7th graders, I have spoken in front of hundreds of children, yet, in all of these roles I was practicing my vibrational field, how I felt about my Energy, and how much fun I was having. At 60 years young I will share with you that I love being on the other side of the camera and teaching, speaking, guiding, most of all challenging you to look outside your box.

So, next time you're struggling in a career, getting upset with yourself because it's not working, remember you are practicing. Practice does not make perfect. Practice makes permanent behavior. Feeling adventure and enthusiasm for what you do to make money will help you connect to your true personal power.

When you're feeling stuck, that's when you raise your Energy in 30 seconds or less naturally to change that pattern that neural loop in your brain. Do the Shine on Shake to disrupt that Energy and keep going with positivity, your passion, your career, your work, your money maker!

When I first started producing my TV shows, they were challenging. Many times, I could not even watch myself. Yet, I kept saying to myself, "You're practicing, Angel. You'll get it; you'll get it. You'll find a flow; keep at it!" So now, after four seasons of producing the TV shows, I feel I give value and great golden nuggets that help others change their life. Every TV show is an exciting adventure now!

Raising your Energy and connecting to your passion for your work will help you naturally show up with enthusiasm and wonder.

On-the-Job Energy

Does your job serve you? Do you go home happy and energized? Are you happy to go to work? Are you looking for a new job?

Studies show that there are many people who only stay in their job for less than a year. Resources also showed that people want to feel that they are giving to humanity and making a difference in the world.

You want to have a career you love so that your Energy will boost naturally, and you will feel better after a day of work. One of my friends who is 92 years old said that he was still working because he did not want to desert his clients and should have retired 7 or 8 years ago. Do you feel like you're staying in a job because you owe it to someone? Maybe you work at a family business or it's your best friend's. You are not alone.

I had a Tai Chi student ask me how to interact at work to make it more positive. "First of all," I told her, "Check your Energy and stay positive yourself. Understand this: when you are at work you are performing, as an actress, either learning or serving others. So, here's one way to get through your day and make it a fun experience.

I want you to think about the other people who are at your work and how you interact. Think about how sometimes it can be frustrating, and you may struggle with the inconsistencies of your co-workers or the ones you serve. That's why it's important to always check your Energy for balance and alignment.

Raising your Energy in 30 seconds or less naturally can Ignite your passion at your current job or Ignite your passion for your dream job.

Phone Energy

Do you like being on the phone. Are you and your phone joined at the hip? Do you have a land line?

Studies show that 86% of people globally have smart phones. According to recent data, the average person spends between 3-5 hours a day on their phone. Also, they check their phone almost 100 times a day. These studies are staggering to me because of the Energy of not only the cell phone itself, yet the accumulated Energy of all those personal interactions.

Today everyone, even children, have phones with them constantly. They keep us connected and keep us safe and provide entertainment. We use our cell phones to keep in touch with loved ones, and for many the phone is essential for work.

Yet, there is growing evidence that radiation from our phones may cause harm to our bodies. Also, many of us spend too much time using our phones when we could be exercising or creating something we are passionate about.

One way to deal with cell phones radiation is to distance yourself by using speaker phone when it's practical. Put the phone down 10 feet away from your body between calls. Many use the cell phone as an alarm. I recommend you get rid of the phone completely while you sleep.

Another way of dealing with cell phone radiation is to spend time in nature so that it Ignites your own healing Energy. I've heard that nature is the original healer. I like that because I feel when I go outside, I can breathe in the desert, and the desert has as much comfort and healing Energy as the forest.

Imagine being in an office cubicle working away, yet while you are staring into the computer and typing away, you start to take deep breaths and visualize yourself in nature.

Feel the flow and the ease of the Energy as the wind and the fresh smell of nature fills you with healing Energy.

When sitting down to eat, silence your phone and remove it from the table, or leave it in another room. Let the Energy from your meal Ignite your senses and nourish your day.

Raising your Energy in 30 seconds or less naturally helps you to distance yourself from the phone.

Social Media Energy

Are you on social media? Do you have a social media account? Are you on multiple platforms? Is social media a blessing or a curse to you?

One study showed that wanting to fit in or the fear of being left out is why social media is so popular. Also, people want to stay in touch with family and friends. Yet, another study proved that social media is addictive because it triggers the brain's reward system and releases that "feel-good" chemical. Other research found that the average person spends over 40% of their time on social media either creating, commenting, scrolling or watching other people's lives.

Social media can suck your Energy and time away to nothing, or it can be the best-ever marketing platform and social connection with family and friends!

At one of my speaking engagements after I finished my presentation an attendee told me he appreciated the teaching about time blocking. He continued to say that he felt he was being sucked in with social media and didn't realize how much time he was spending scrolling. He also added that he was going to create a schedule to have less screen time and more interaction with others and himself. I congratulated him on taking a positive step for change that would help him experience more positive Energy.

Another one of the attendees who is also a counseling client shared with us her experience with time blocking. She said by implementing time blocking and only posting four times a week instead of everyday she noticed the same amount interaction. She was so thankful she learned this process and felt she had more Energy and clarity throughout the day.

Many of my fellow professional speakers use social media to reach people worldwide with their heartfelt messages and services. Social media is a valuable communication tool that I use to share positive Energy, hope, and inspiration.

So, next time you are on social media raise your Energy in 30 seconds or less naturally and show up with kindness and support.

Action Step from the SHINE ON! book

Breathe... If you are seated for more than an hour set a timer. When the timer goes off get up and move for at least ten minutes. This is not the time to get on the phone or check social media. And breathe...

Networking Energy

Do you like social events? Have you ever been to a networking event? Do you look forward to making new connections at networking events?

Recent data says that many people spend 5 to 6 hours a week in some networking activity. Approximately half are there because they feel networking will make their business successful.

Networking has a vibration all to its own. The Energy of networking can be a mishmash of fear, desperation and lack. This Energy of hopelessness, worry and self-doubt can be present within ourselves and others. On an energetic level this can feel heavy. I know. I can feel it because I am an empath and highly connected to the energies around people. Networking can be fun and is very valuable. Here is one way to raise your Energy and be able to share your passion, your purpose, your business with high Energy and enthusiasm.

I hug you when I meet you. So, I am in your Energy field. I step back and clap my hands softly a couple of times to clear your Energy and ground mine. People look at me and say, "Oh, you're so cute, you're adorable, oh my gosh!" Yet, I clap after hugging anyone, even my Mama, because you want to keep your Energy clear and balanced. Clapping is a powerful tool to use anytime, anywhere, to release unwanted Energy and Ignite your abundance.

Raising your Energy in 30 seconds or less naturally by clapping can help you to reboot your Energy.

Chapter 6 Finance Energy

Money is Energy and your Energy is very valuable just like money. Money holds Energy not only by being physically dirty, it's also a mishmash of human emotions, vibrational fields in the lower energies of greed, grief, depression and longing.

Money can also be represented as a social power. Money gives you the freedom to do what you want, be who you want and go where you want. Without money, you may feel like you have fewer options, decreased personal fulfillment and freedom.

"Lack is an illusion. There are always more crayons to create your world."
~ Angel Marie

Money Energy

Would you like to have more money? Do you think about money often? Would you like to be a millionaire? Do you like the feel of $100 bills in your hand?

Studies show that having more money leads to higher life satisfaction however, ironically, it does not buy happiness, emotional well-being, or love. Another study revealed that people who make less are more generous than people who make more. When you spend money on things you can afford and that makes you happy, that's when the Energy of money becomes happiness and joy.

Many years ago, I remember at Lightworkers Gifts Energy Healing Center a Master teacher was teaching a seminar, and he asked the most puzzling question. "If money were a human and walked through the door what would money say about your relationship?" Back then I did not understand how to answer the question and just blew it off. Yet now it is a huge part of what I teach. All Energy can be transformed to limitless possibilities and making a friend of money is transformative.

Remember, you are in control of your money. Use it as the means to better your own life and the lives of those around you. Our thoughts, our words and our emotions are impacted by the give and take of money. The process is simple. To get what you want, you trade money (Energy) for the value (Energy) of something else.

Health is our new wealth, and many times we burn out by pushing so hard to acquire money that we diminish or self-sabotage our own health. Money provides comfort and joy and is a form of Energy, just like water. Flowing with money and not hoarding money creates more money!

A good friend and spiritual leader shared with me that giving is receiving in another Energy form. She also added that when you transfer your Energy from your material bank account to a good karma account you create blessings and a wonderful way to serve others.

Choose a way of giving that is personal to you, and the love you have for money and the essence of that love will reach the people, organization, or non-profit you are giving to.

It's OK to say, "Thank you, money," and give gratitude for money just as you do for all your other blessings.

Raise your Energy in 30 seconds or less naturally by giving thanks and making friends with your money!

Manifesting Money Energy

Are your thoughts and actions driven by money? Do you want to manifest more money? Do you feel limited in the amount of money you can make?

Studies have shown that negative mood or attitude pulls your Energy down. People who are generally happy and positive attract more opportunities, have better relationships, and are usually more successful. Energy vibrates at different frequencies, and research shows these frequencies can sync up and begin to resonate within each other. That's what manifesting feels like. It feels like you're in sync with the world and your desires.

Like Energy becomes Like Energy. Whatever vibrational field you put around you is what you will attract. That's quantum physics. That's one of the laws of the universe and the universe is all Energy! So, manifesting is understanding that when you desire something, for example, money, you manifest it by using your thoughts, feelings and beliefs to bring that to your physical reality.

There is a fair amount of science behind the idea of manifestation. One research showed that believing you can do something makes it more likely that you actually will do that thing. This may seem vague, yet the research showed that when you truly believe you can achieve something, you are willing to put in the work. And the key to manifesting what you want, what you need, what you believe you can do is to feel strongly enough about it to be persistent, and ultimately engage in the behavior that brings about the outcome you desire. When you have inspired action, you see and feel when and how to take the action.

One of the keys to manifesting anything in your life is to get clear on exactly what you want to manifest. If you're struggling to see your desires clearly, be gentle with yourself and spend some time focusing on getting clarity. Create a space for mindful meditation and using breathing to quiet the mind so that it will help to increase self-awareness. Also, Ignite play and have some fun with a vision board, cutting pictures out and writing down words that will help you be in the Energy of what you desire.

Having a clear Energy field to bring in an abundance of money takes time to reprogram your neural nets in the brain to break old loops. You may be in the field of, "I am not worthy," or "I am fearful of success." Remember, F.E.A.R. is Fresh Energy Accepting Realignment. That is why it is powerful when you raise your Energy naturally around money and watch how opportunities come out of nowhere.

Watch how unexpected money shows up in your bank account. Thank the money! Say, "Thank you! I'm so glad that I can take this money, pay a bill or go shopping and have fun with the natural Energy of limitless abundance."

A client reminded me at Lightworkers Gifts Energy Healing Center of an abundance meditation class. The Master Teacher had us go into a meditation and put millions of dollars in a pile as big or small as we wanted. She had us breathe excitement into the pile of money and feel the joy of the money. Then she said to set it on fire!

That instant was when I understood about Energy and that everything is ENERGY. My whole body and my emotions felt comatose. I did not want to blow up all the money. I also recognized how much I was coming from a lack mentality about money and how my thoughts, emotions, and beliefs about money were negative. I felt angry and frustrated. I struggled with a feeling of scarcity. This helped me to open my eyes to really understanding that the universe is limitless and so is money!

Manifesting money is about putting your Energy into the clarity of what you want, setting goals, and generally feeling optimistic about reaching the goals. So, shift your Energy and change your thoughts, emotions, and actions now!

Action Step from the SHINE ON! Book

Breathe... Before you get out of bed say three times "I have all that I desire and I am abundant." And breathe...

I encourage you. I implore you. I challenge you. I invite you, and I kick you with love, to spend time in the imagination of serving millions, making millions, giving away millions, and having fun with all the details.

Raise your Energy in 30 seconds or less naturally with the feeling and knowing you have limitless millions in your bank account!

Paying Bills Energy

Do you have a specific time every week you pay bills? Do you struggle to get up and pay bills? Do you pay by check or online? Are bills and paying them a top priority? Do you sometimes forget to pay bills and then have to pay a late charge?

A brief survey with my Reiki students revealed that more than 70% of them looked at paying bills as a negative. There are many different systems and practices of how you pay your bills. Studies show that we learned our system from our parents, and that more than half the population feels a lack mentality when paying bills.

It's interesting because money is Energy, and if you don't mindfully appreciate money, you are telling money and your bills that you are not worthy. Instead, appreciate having the money to pay the bills and celebrate as you pay them. Give thanks to money, raise your Energy, and Ignite your consciousness of abundance. It's a joyous way to pay the bills!

Being active in the Energy of moving money, flowing money outward as money flows inwards, is a yin and yang activity. Embracing both is called appreciating the money going out. When you feel deserving and grateful when paying for your electricity, and the events you attend, you also embrace and feel grateful for the money that comes in.

Giving thanks to money is a concept that most people are not taught. At one of the Shine On Saturdays at Energy Empowerment Hour I asked the group, "How many of you give thanks to your car, house and things that you have?" Everyone said, "Yes!" Then I asked, "how many of you gave thanks to the money to pay for these things?" Not one person said yes… wow!

Here is one of the best ways to energetically stay organized and pay your bills on time and joyously.

One of my guests on the *Your Time to Shine International Interview Series* shared this with us: write the name and due date of your bills on a calendar. After you pay each bill, write "Thank you money, Thank you Higher Self/God/Universe, Thank you and (fill in your name)." Then the final piece is raising your Energy by celebrating paying the bill. This is absolutely brilliant: feel the Energy around writing it out and giving thanks.

So, crank up *The Shine On Song* on Pandora or Spotify, get moving and connect to the feeling of the flow as you click away and pay bills, or you write out bills. Do it with appreciation, laughter, and joy.

Raise your Energy in 30 seconds or less naturally and get excited to pay those bills!

Saving Money

Are you a saver? Do you have a savings account? Is saving money something you strive for yet never really achieve?

Research shows that many people feel more stable and in control when they have a savings account. I really believe this is a generational thing because I have seen it in my counseling clients of different age groups. For my generation, the practice of tithing was taught to us. It was ingrained in us to do the right thing and give back. Different generations have different ideas of what's right or wrong regarding money.

A study showed that over 70% of the American people have a savings account. I believe that is due to a belief system in our Energy which says we should always make sure that we have enough saved for a rainy day, or reserves that can even go for food and utilities.

I'm going to be very transparent here. I visualize the flow of money daily. I choose to put money back into my business, into my passion, which is to share my message and serve millions of people. I always know that the flow of incoming clients, speaking engagements, book sales, and so much more is limitless.

So, maybe your parents or a good book taught you that you should save money. One system I use is, when money comes in, I put a percentage of it in my savings account.

Raise your Energy in 30 seconds or less naturally to Ignite your visualization of saving money.

Abundance and Gratitude Story

This is a true story about when I owned Lightworkers Gifts Energy Healing Center and I had no money. The mortgage was due, my dog needed food, and so did I.

I went outside and sat and said, "Okay Higher Self/God/Universe, if you still want me to be here serving others with self-care, self-development and having a safe place for people to gather and look at themselves in a different perspective, bring me the money or I'm closing the Center and filing bankruptcy and getting a real job."

Within 30 minutes I had three new counseling and Reiki clients that paid the bills for the rest of the month. I knew I manifested that because, not only did I ask to be shown, I asked to be in service to help others. Every time I have been in a place where the lack mentality of money Energy started to fill my essence, I went back to what I know to be true: I deserve the very best. I have a message. I serve millions. I went back to my commitment, my knowing that everyone on the planet wants to be happy and harmonious and they are loving.

You are loving, powerful, and strong. Nothing exists outside of you. There's only the inner knowing that it is our birthright to have abundance.

Chapter 7 Humanity Energy

Are you seeing humanity and the world in a negative or positive way? Are you worried about what is going on in the world? Do you sometimes feel completely horrified about what is happening in the world?

"Inspire integrity by choosing honest thoughts and actions."
~ Angel Marie

World events are so heavy at times my clients say they feel frozen or stuck. Here is a common denominator with all humans in the world: No matter how far apart we are in miles we all have EMOTIONS. What happens in faraway places against humanity, against nature, against Mother Earth, against animals, against races, against LGBTQs, against kids, and, sadly, against so much more, the emotional Energy of events affects us all.

This chapter had to be here to remind us of our resilience and courage. Also, to experience the collective oneness of Energy and the realization that through Mother Earth and quantum physics we all vibe together with emotions.

We all are related to each other, no matter what the demographics are, just as the galaxies in the universe are related. Furthermore, believing that this planet has a purpose, and YOU have a purpose helps you accept the tender, sensitive, and compassionate parts of humanity.

With the highest of appreciation for all humanity I feel it is a privilege to be alive right now, to be part of the Energy on this planet, to see how humanity is changing, transforming, and rising up. I have heard kindness is the new cool. I love that, and that's really cool!

Open your heart and feel your Higher Self/God/Universe. Do the Shine On Shake, and release to activate your divine life commitment, passion, and purpose in this world. The kids are our future, so always nurture them.

Bottom line, stay in your own lane, don't judge, and Ignite joy always. Your function is to be a happy human!

Thank you for shining your light with love, grace, healing, gratitude, and joy! Always be safe and feel safe, secure, and protected!

A Personal Thank You!

Congratulations! I'm so excited that you have chosen to claim your personal Energy and raise your vibration so that you have more confidence, joy, and abundance in your life!

I hope the invitations and golden nuggets in this book have served to bring more inspiration and playfulness into your life. Whenever you need a little inspiration or encouragement, come back to these chapters, and shift your perspective and Energy.

And always remember to Ignite your Energy and Shine On!

Thank you,

Angel Marie

Appreciation and Gratitude

My deepest appreciation to my Higher Self/God/Universe for allowing me to Ignite my passion and see my purpose in the brightest light. Energy is light and I am grateful that I am able to serve others with the gifts I have been given. So, say this with me, "When I Ignite my gifts, I Ignite my power!"

To My Mama: Thank you for always trusting me enough to give me the freedom to make choices for myself and always encouraging me to dream big. Thanks for being my Mama and loving me so much.

You are a gift beyond measure Barbara Anderson! You are my friend, Reiki student and soul sister. Thank you for your selfless act of gifting me the ability to share my message with the world. I am forever grateful!

My deepest gratitude to my fellow soul brother in spirit for being my guide in the ultimate dream to sing and have a signature song. You resonate healing Energy, FiZ Anthony! Your genius helped me set the tone of Shine Energy.

Susan Hutchins, you are one of the most connected, insightful and knowledgeable Energy Healers I know. I am honored to call you my best friend and thank you for the countless hours where you have talked me off the cliff and healed me up!

Nancy Blum Urbach, my rock, my soul sister, you inspire me and humble me. Thank you, my dear sister friend, for YOU!

Donna Smith, my amazing Reiki student, soul sister, friend, and beautician, thank you for reminding me to laugh, have fun and value my gifts. I cherish our beauty parties.

Tricia Francis Bowman my dear soul sister words cannot express how thankful I am that you saved my life that hot summer day at the cliffs. You are a divine light in my world, and I am blessed by you.

To Linda Mardel, my friend and Reiki student, your patience and compassion during the editing of this book helped me create a space of divine creativity. Thank you for your amazing gifts.

To Rita Bojorquez for all the years of the amazing healing sessions and messages that have changed my life. I am blessed by you and thank you for always believing in me.

My amazing, gifted friend and soul sister, my admiration for you Dr. Sony Jackson is enormous. You are a truly gifted writer, and I am blessed by how you have helped me express myself more fully. Thank you for all the encouragement and love.

To my awesome, gifted friend and personal marketing genius, Preston Martelly. From the moment I met you, I fell into gratitude for you. Your brilliant ninja tricks and tools are invaluable. Thank you for always supporting and loving me.

Universal gratitude to Robert and Shawn Jones, the founders of INETrepreneur Network, and their community for supporting my vision and light. You are an amazing group of connectors!

To Emilio and Daniela Roman founders of Author Millionaire Academy a heartfelt thank you for your vision and mission. Your unending support and love are cherished. Blessed to be part of a community that is so inspiring and encouraging. Your love helped to keep me going and stay focused. With laughter! Thank you, AMA family!

To my Reiki students, I have limitless gratitude for keeping me humble, always nurturing me and giving me the greatest joy of all being your Reiki Master/Teacher friend.

To the Saturday morning Tai Chi family my deepest thank you for honoring the Energy and pouring love and light into the world. You are truly a gift to me!

To my family at the Shine On Saturdays Meetup, thank you for your fun, insights, and awesome connections. Always look forward to Saturdays with YOU!

Don McGrath and Jim Grant, Founders of the Scale Pathway and Six Minute Webinar, your expertise has been invaluable to me. Thank you for your ongoing friendship, coaching and business knowledge.

Special appreciation for the cover picture from my dear friend and soul sister Stephanie Westover of ValWestoverPhotoGraphy.com

To all my TV Show Guests past and present thank you for showing up and giving from the heart!

Heartfelt thank you and respect for you Lynn Murphy! So honored to be one of the women in your book "50 Life Lessons from Inspiring Women." You are a blessing in my life!

I am where I am today because of your friendship, partnership, healing, and motivation DJ Khamis, Elena & Jim Thornton, Coach Sherry Winn, Leslie Swann, Sophia Olivas, Krystylle Richardson, Israel Mandrake, Julie "Juju" Christopher, Aaron Heimes, Leslie Lempka, Bruce Serbin, Tim Burt, Andrew Ecker, Janine Kesselman, Terri Pilato Zbick, Beverly Brown, Mandy Robinson, Joan Ellen Pearlman, Larry Weinberg, Myoshi Maul. Thank you!

Special Thank you to Team Angel: Linda Mardel, Tricia Francis Bowman, Mahogonee Mcintyre, Preston Martelly, Dr. Sony Jackson, Lyn De Leaon-De Vera, Marjorie Duarte.

To all the past, present, and future people who have believed in me helped me, supported me, loved me, guided me, cried with me, and partied with me, to name a few, and I'm sure I have missed many: Vinny Dileo, Jill Wieman, Lisa Norveen, Camille Robb, Austin J. Haines, Maureen Zachondiak Dourlaris.

Appreciation for every person I have connected with through counseling, readings, and healing sessions at Lightworkers Gifts Energy Healing Center.

Heartfelt thanks to you who have embraced and shared the SHINE ON! book and its philosophy.

Much love and thank you to my family, friends, and social media connections for your support.

For all of those unnamed, know that you reside in my heart, and I am grateful for how you showed up in my life.

Special appreciation for you who pre-ordered this book, it is evidence of your belief in me and this message.

Special Free Gift for You

If your eyes have been opened to the world of Ignited Energy and you would like to continue the adventure, give yourself permission to enjoy these gifts and raise your Energy with more confidence, joy and abundance.

Special FREE Bonus Gift for YOU

Get your 3 FREE in-depth training videos on
How to Ignite Your Shine On Energy,
Attract more Confidence, Joy and Abundance!

www.FreeGiftfromAngelMarie.com

For daily inspiration, join me on YouTube

https://YouTube.com/AngelMarieShines

Other Books By Angel Marie

 SHINE ON!: 52 Secrets for Greater Success and Higher Self-Esteem

Your Amazing Itty Bitty Book of Words: 270 Words to Educate and Entertain Your Mind

 Women Who Push the Limits Presents: 50 Life Lessons From Inspiring Women

The Art of Connection: 365 Days of Networking Quotes by Entrepreneurs, Business Owners and Influencers

 The Art Of Connection: 365 Days of Inspirational Quotes by Entrepreneurs, Business Owners, and Influencers

Spiritual Fitness Survivor: How To Turn Your Struggles Into Strength 3rd Edition

available on Amazon.com

Energize Your Next Event

Have you noticed that people are not "fully present" and engaged at events?

Angel Marie works with event planners, hosts, and speakers to create an energizing, educational and engaging event.

Angel Marie has an absolutely infectious energy that infuses any online or in-person event with enthusiasm, passion and fun! She is the perfect "event energizer" because she personally connects with the participants, and creates excitement and enthusiasm for the event. I saw Angel in action first-hand and she energized, engaged and educated the audience of more than 200 women with fun and memorable discussions and interactions, which allowed the participants to have more clarity and focus during the event.

Linda Fisk
Founder and CEO at LeadHERship Global

Book Angel Marie
Angel Marie Monachelli
24 W. Camelback Rd, Ste A-413
Phoenix, AZ 85013
(623) 334-3393
Angel@AngelMarieShines.com
www.ShineOnWithAngel.com

**RAISE YOUR ENERGY IN 30
SECONDS OR LESS NATURALLY**

CHANGE YOUR MINDSET

IGNITE YOUR LIFE

S H I N E   O N !

#IGNITEBOOK
#SHINEONWITHANGEL

Made in the USA
Monee, IL
28 January 2023

26573173R00066